I0467288

Table of Contents

INTRODUCTION

Introduction

➢ Fiverr V2 has delivered more tools and capabilities to both sellers and buyers, making the process of creating Gigs and purchasing not only easy, but simple and fun.

➢ I will share with you in this step by step e-book the top unrevealed realistic formulas to live in the kingdom of Fiverr, whether you are a seller and/or a buyer, beginner or advanced.

Who This E-book is For?

Sellers	Buyers
• Who want to rank their Gigs in Fiverr & Google • Who want to boost their sales & dominate their niche • Who want to learn how to deal with hard buyers and keep the 100% rating • Who are offering great Gigs and they are still waiting for orders	• We are human, and we know that we cannot be the best in every domain, but actually we can do that now with Fiverr ☺: the formula is simple, all you need to do is choose the best sellers to do your jobs for you, and then you are gonna be the best. This e-book will guide

• Who are new and don't know where or how to start in the kingdom of Fiverr • Who are looking for inspiration for new Gigs • Who want to discover the top Gigs secrets	you to find the right sellers that are able to do your jobs, and without wasting your money or your time on the wrong sellers.

➤ This e-book contains all the tips, techniques and strategies that I have collected from my experience and from the Top Rated Sellers on Fiverr and that I have tested and used for a long time, **I have held nothing back, and in this e-book I share with you ALL of my lighting secrets and techniques.**

➤ This is a clear, structured, kept simple & short and to the point e-book ☺.

➤ The Fiverr V2 Kingdom Formula is a **"MUST E-BOOK"** for any seller and/or buyer on Fiverr.

GETTING STARTED WITH FIVERR V2

What is & Why Fiverr

What is Fiverr

✓ Fiverr is the world's largest marketplace for small services.

✓ The website was founded by Micha Kaufman and Shai Wininger, and it was launched in February 2010.

✓ The website transaction volume has grown 600% since 2011.

7

Why Fiverr

✓ Fiverr is one of the best ways to start making money on the Internet.

✓ Many of sellers have left their day job, because they can make more money with Fiverr.

✓ According to Fiverr.com's blog:

  ➢ **14% of sellers** already report Fiverr as their **primary source of income.**

  ➢ **15% of sellers** have earned **+$1,000 | 27%** have earned **+$500 | 57%** have earned **+$100**.

✓ The huge amount of traffic that Fiverr receive will help ensure that you get several sales for your products or services.

✓ Fiverr's visitors are targeted visitors who are willing to spend money on Fiverr, and even those who go to Fiverr to make money end up spending money there.

✓ It's much harder to sell information than it is to sell a service, and here comes Fiverr.

✓ We all know that as we are humans, no one can do everything at once or be the best at everything, but with Fiverr you can ☺ , how? Just hire the right sellers on Fiverr to do your job, and that's it.

Create your Fiverr Account

✓ **Username:**

➤ I believe it is a good idea to choose a username that reflects your service in Fiverr; I think it's gonna be better than a random username that may mean something to you, but means nothing to the buyers. I mean by random usernames, usernames like:

- suuzy18; sep_147; sosteen588

And I mean by usernames that reflect your service, usernames like:

- YourCompany; YourService;

✓ **Your profile picture:**

➤ Put up a picture. I don't know why, but when your profile is without a picture, I feel, it says "Hi buyers I am a newbie ☺"

➤ Having a real photo of a seller gives you more credibility. Also, a real photo adds a personal touch, and people like to know who they are dealing with.

➤ Or you can just use a graphic that represents your service on Fiverr;

✓ **Something about you:**

➢ Ensure that you have taken the time to add at least a few sentences about yourself or your business that you plan on having on Fiverr.

Around a Gig

✓ Here's some points to keep in mind before you create a new Gig:

1) Think about hobbies and talents that you can offer as a service. Take this opportunity to do what you love and make it your business.

2) Your Gig should be relatively easy for you to complete.

3) Do some research to see if you have competitors for the service you want to offer on Fiverr. Check out what they are offering and if your service and quality is competitive. Also, if you have a unique advantage be sure to highlight it in your Gig description.

4) Your description should clearly explain your service to buyers. Include details of what you do and what you don't do.

5) Always change your delivery time according to the number of orders you have. Because once the orders start coming in, you'll need to be able to keep up and complete them on time.

6) Optimize your title, description and tags with keywords, because that's important for Search Engine Optimization inside and outside Fiverr.

7) Add a video that introduces yourself and/or your service to the buyers.

8) The more Gigs you have, the better your chances of getting sales.

I think every seller can have up to 20 Gigs, and the Top Rated Sellers can have up to 30 Gigs.

Inspiration for New Gigs

✓ There is no limit on Fiverr, you can create Gigs about almost anything you can imagine, the possibilities are endless.

✓ Write down ALL what you are very good at.

✓ Look at the different Gigs that are already created on Fiverr for inspiration.

✓ Remember, Fiverr is an incredibly popular platform nowadays, which means that you're going to find it difficult to come up with a Gig idea that's entirely unique. However if you can't come up with this kind of Gigs, then look at a number of Gigs that are providing the same service that you want to offer, and see how much they offer for $5, the types of Gig extras they offer, and their delivery time. All of these points are going to be important factors when you will design your own Gig.

SELLERS

Tips for Sellers

✓ **Title:**

> ➤ Make sure your title is short, clear and to the point.

> ➤ You are only allowed 1 capitalized word on your title, so it's gonna be a good idea to CAPITALIZE your main KEYWORD.

> ➤ Pick a creative, Specific, and eye CATCHING title.

✓ **Video Gig:**

> ➤ People LOVE videos. Most people hate reading, I hate reading :
>
> Create a video with either yourself explaining your service or create a video showcasing your work/what you do. And if you are stuck, just hire someone on Fiverr to do your video Gig for you.

> ➤ In the video tell the buyers exactly **what** they should do, **how** they should do it, and **what** they can **expect**.

> ➤ A video Gig can save you writing long paragraphs in your Gig's description

✓ **Portfolio:**

> ➤ Your portfolio is turned on by default when you create a new Gig on Fiverr.

➢ Your Portfolio avoid negative feedbacks or cancellations, simply because the buyers know what to expect, as they have an idea from the samples from your portfolio.

➢ So let's see now how to show services that are not videos or images on your portfolio:

- If your deliver audio, make a video with your audio and any related picture.
- If you deliver applications, make screenshots of your final application.
- If you deliver something else, just think about it and you will find definitely some way to get your works on your portfolio.

Finally you will deliver 2 files: your audio/application etc. and also a video or picture to your buyer. So don't forget to mention to your buyer that the video or the picture is just for your portfolio so he or she is not confused.

✓ **Gig's Description**:

➢ Provide clear instructions to the buyers. Because if you do this correctly, it will save you a considered amount of time answering unnecessary messages from some buyers.

➢ Create smaller Gig's description, simply because most of the buyers don't read descriptions when they are lonnnng and they may just order your Gig, and that may lead to negative reviews or cancellations. I know you have a lot to say, but less is truly more. The longer your Gig's description, the less chance it will be read.

➢ Also, make sure to take advantage of the new Gig's description features in Fiverr V2, to make your Gig's description more clear.

➢ Finally, here's my personal powerful format for Gig's description:

1) **Introduce your service and yourself (optional, introduce yourself only if it is related to your service)**
2) **Input**
3) **Output**
4) **Extra description (optimized with Keywords), this is very important for SEO (Search Engine Optimization)**

✓ Gig Extras:

➢ Break your service up into many jobs starting with a basic but complete service at $5. And for each extra service, you can charge more.

- In your Gig's description, you can explain in more details what the buyers can get for some extras if they are not clear enough.

- If you don't know what to offer in your Gig extras, think about services that someone buying your Gig may need.

- Your Gig Extras MUST be something WIN for the buyers, they should feel like they will miss it if they don't order this extra.

- So always make your Gig Extras attractive deals to the buyers.

- Always promote your Gig Extras. Let the buyers know about your Extras when you are chatting with them before and after they place the order.

- When you have many orders, set your Gig to be completed for example by 4 or even a week, and offer the **Extra Fast** feature, and people will pay you Extra to get their orders done fast.

- Based on your experience with your specific Gigs, always think of new ways to use the Extra Features.

✓ **Express Gigs:**

Express service attracts buyers

➤ If you can **'Express your Gig'** then express it! Because that will result in more orders.

➤ Actually, people like speed and quality work, and that is the reason why Fiverr has added this feature to sort the search results.

✓ **Delivery Time:**

➤ Do not do a rush job and deliver poor work just to meet a deadline. In the event that you think you are going to be late, it is always a good idea to contact the buyer and request a small extension of a few hours or a day or more, and tell him/her **WHY** you need that extra time.

➤ Try always to complete your orders and to deliver them as soon as possible no matter what your delivery time says, in other words **clear your queue** as soon as you can, and buyers will appreciate it.

➤ Shorten the delivery time as lowest as you can, because this is important to increase the number of orders.

✓ **Fiverr's Levels:**

➢ Level flags are a major factor in whether a buyer will click on your Gig or someone else's. Just having that Top Rated Seller flag against your name is enough to get you chosen by many buyers instead of others, so the Fiverr's levels are really important in the Fiverr Kingdom.

✓ **Discounts:**

➢ Offering discounts is not only a great way to attract more customers, but it also helps to sell more Gigs per customer. If someone needs a lot of content then make your Gig save him/her some money. Also, it's a way of saying "thank you" to the buyers that put their trust in you as a seller and buy in bulk.

✓ **Communication:**

➢ Prepare **Reply ready documents** including answers to the FAQ that buyers usually ask you, so you don't have to start writing the same answers every time, instead you will just need to copy and paste. And don't forget to keep updating your **reply ready documents** as more questions arise and as you create more Gigs. Also remember to personalize them for each buyer.

- ➤ By recommending other Gigs that your buyers may need, your buyers will remember you.
- ➤ Reply to everyone:
  - • Daily many orders, comments and questions are received. Sometimes some messages seem "silly" and "uninformative" and might not catch the attention. In spite of their content, I recommend to answer to ALL the messages, because you don't know from where potential customers may show up.
- ➤ Reply on time:
  - • Answer messages right away, do not leave them on "a little later". The perfect time is NOW not "a little later"
- ➤ Show it:
  - • There are situations when the client misunderstand, or miss something, so don't be lazy to make screenshots for clarity. It's a matter of seconds, with a possible income.
- ➤ Bonus:

- Loyal clients are gold to us! Like everyone they like to be appreciated: so be generous, and give them bonuses.

➢ Try to leave feedback to all your customers too - We all expect to get a positive feedback, but I've noticed that there are many sellers that do not care anymore for their buyers after getting a positive feedback.

➢ if you get a Gig order that requests something more than you can handle, be honest with the buyer and let him/her know that, and these are some magic words that firmly say "no thank you":

- "To be completely honest with you, this is out of my capabilities right now, but what I can do for you is this [describe concretely what you can do]."

- "Thanks, but I think that is beyond what I am offering. I hope you can find someone else for the job"

- "I understand your request, however, at this time, I do not offer to do that service."

✓ **Over Delivery**

➢ Always do your best, whether the customer is a returning or a new customer.

➢ Always give your buyer more than what is written, because when the buyer is happy:

- He/she will give you a positive review.
- It's more likely that he/she will choose you rather than other sellers the next time.

✓ **Feedback**

➢ Your goal is to maintain the 100% (not 99%) feedback rating, so do what you need to do to keep your rating perfect.

➢ **1** negative feedback can make many buyers stay away from your Gig.

➢ I think with a rating under 80%, you will find it hard to get someone to order from you, so you should always try to find out where is the problem with the buyer and correct it.

➢ You don't know how many buyers you lose when they see negative reviews, and you know what, personally when I see a Gig reviews I look only for those negative reviews to read what those buyers said.

- ➤ If the buyer didn't leave a feedback he is usually a new buyer in Fiverr, or some buyers may think you do not need it, and some are just lazy. So be proactive, and always ask the buyers to leave a positive feedback for you and tell them why.

Here are some message models I send to my buyers whenever I deliver any order, and that most of the times result in positive reviews:

- • "If you're happy with the work please be sure to leave a positive review."
- • "If there are any problems then please let me know. Otherwise, I would really appreciate it if you would take the time to leave a positive feedback."
- • "Kindly COMMENT on my Gig, I would really appreciate it ;)"
- • "One last thing...

  Kindly leave a positive feedback in the feedback box below. It's really important, my Fiverr standing depends on it :)"
- ➤ As a seller, don't get mad and more importantly, do not leave the buyer a negative feedback, this will just fuel

the fire. Always contact the buyer to see exactly what the problem was, and based on his/her reply, you'll know how to move forward.

> If a buyer leaves you a negative feedback and he/she doesn't want to remove it whatever you did. Just state the facts in your review, be positive and be graceful, because other buyers will be watching you.

> Converting unhappy customers into happy customers:

  • Although it doesn't happen often, sometimes a client will not like your outcome. When this happens, **that client should immediately moves up to the top of your priority list**. Ask the buyer to tell you what he/she didn't like exactly, then try to fix it according to his/her requirements. Keep working on the order until the customer is 100% happy. If the buyer is still not happy after this revision process, ask for mutual cancellation.

> But hey, wait a second, **the customer is NOT always right**: if you feel that you have received a negative feedback that is not justified, just contact the Fiverr Customer Support to get it removed.

✓ As a no level seller, it may take you a few hours, days, weeks or even months to get your first customer, just don't give up! It's always a little slow when you are brand new, but once you get rolling, you'll start having more orders than you know what to do with ☺.

✓ Remember also that sales may start super slow, but they will pick up eventually! So patience is a big part in the kingdom of Fiverr.

✓ Actually, buyers often choose sellers who have tons of positive feedbacks, and that's normal, because you would do the same yourself if you want to buy a Gig from Fiverr, wouldn't you? ☺

✓ Also remember, you're building a strong foundation for a long-term profitable business, so the extra effort is necessary, especially at the beginning.

✓ **"Buyer Requests" list:**

   ➢ Personally this is where I got my first orders.

   ➢ When you answer the buyers' requests, make sure to watch your inbox, because buyers want their requests immediately, so if you do not answer your inbox quickly, the buyer may go to the next sellers.

Personally I use the **Checker Plus for Gmail™** extension in Google Chrome to get instant notification once I get a new message.

➤ New Fiverr sellers: Do not deliver any buyer request without the buyer purchasing your Gig first. Actually, new sellers usually make this mistake.

✓ **Gig Extras:**

➤ Are you a no level seller and you want to offer Gig extras?

• The answer is simple, all you need to do is: use your Gig description to offer your Gig extras.

✓ **Offer more in the beginning:**

➤ Offer a delivery time less than the other sellers to get more orders.

➤ Offer more than what your competitors offer. This will make your service more favorable and cost effective to the buyers.

✓ **Learn new skills:**

➤ We must be honest here. The only way you can make money on Fiverr is if you have skills to perform the jobs. If you lack these specific skills, then try your best and learn the skills that enable you to provide the services you want to offer on Fiverr.

Promote your Gigs:

✓ **Title:**

➢ Title is the most important factor in SEO (Search Engine Optimization), because the Gig's url is made from your title, so make sure to use your main keywords in your Gig's title.

✓ **Video Gig:**

➢ According to Fiverr statistics, sellers who present their service on video, sell 220% more.

➢ If you have a video Gig you will stand with the few sellers who have a video Gig, and then you will increase the exposure of your Gig.

✓ **Description & Tags:**

➢ Make sure to choose the right keywords for your title, description and tags.

➢ Actually, I have noticed that many sellers use only a few tags, and not ALL the allowed number of tags. Because you know what? Every tag you are not using, you are losing orders. Tags are how people find you.

➢ I think you remember my personal powerful formula for the Gig's description I explained earlier in this chapter, and more specifically the part number four. Actually, this extra paragraph will make your Gig show up for the keywords it contains.

✓ **Express Gigs:**

➢ If you can offer your Gig as an Express Gig, then your Gig will show up under the **Express Gigs** feature with the few Gigs that are express.

✓ **Target Specific Sectors:**

➢ Gigs that target specific sectors not only separate you from the competition, but also attract customers who are looking for exactly that solution. The tighter you can narrow your niche, the less competition you face and the more potential customers you attract.

✓ **Social Media (YouTube, Facebook, Twitter, Google+, etc.):**

➢ Participate in Forums discussions related to your Gigs topics while showing your Gigs in your forum signature.

➢ Use your YouTube, Facebook, twitter, Google+, blog, etc. traffic to drive sales to your Gigs.

➢ Upload your video Gig to your YouTube channel. The goal here is to drive people to your YouTube page which then links back to your Fiverr Gig. Because you can have a huge traffic from YouTube, also YouTube videos can show up in Google easily.

✓ Your Mailing Lists:

➢ You can use your own mailing lists to promote your Gigs.

✓ Don't Run against the Storm:

➢ There is a limit on the number of tags you can use, so don't waste them on the tags that are highly competitive. That is really like running against a storm. For example it's really hard to rank for tags like "voice over" or "recording", so instead, use keywords that have low competition and high volume of searches.

➢ When talking about SEO it's all about choosing the right keywords:

▪ Use the new keyword tool of Google: the **Keyword Planner**, and look for the most relevant keywords with low competition and high volume of searches.

I know that this Google keyword tool is for Google and not for Fiverr, but you know what, people use the same keywords they use in Google to search inside Fiverr.

➢ **What To Avoid in SEO**

  ▪ Flooding your title, or your Gig's description with keywords can have a negative impact in Google and Fiverr.

  ▪ Using keywords that are not relevant to your Gigs.

✓ **SEO Link Building**:

➢ It's a well-known fact that links are a very important factor in search engine ranking. Quality links help to strengthen your web pages which increase your search engine position and exposure. This will help you get more traffic.

➢ When done **correctly**, these type of links can really help give your Gig page a boost in search position, so if you don't know how to do backlinks to your Gigs, just hire the right seller from Fiverr to do this for you.

BUYERS

Tips for Buyers

✓ **Before you Order:**

> ➢ Read carefully the Gig's description to see what the seller is really offering, and not only the title ;) .

> ➢ Read the Gig's negative reviews to make sure that you'll not have the same problem(s) with the seller.

> ➢ If you are not really sure if the seller is able or not to do your job, contact him/her first before placing your order.

> ➢ Contact many sellers at the same time to have many offers, then choose the best offer for you.

✓ **Buyer Requests:**

> ➢ Do not just go with the first seller who replies to your request. Shop around, and do some research about the sellers: their level, their Gigs, their reviews, etc.

> ➢ Actually, I have noticed that most of the requests that buyers are requesting exist already in Fiverr, like Voice over, transcription, translation, etc. and even if it doesn't exist in Fiverr you can ask the highly rated sellers who sell in the same category to do your service, and normally they will accept to do it.

So before posting your request, do a Fiverr research of your request and make sure to refine your search results with **High Rating**, this is so important, because you want

Gigs from sellers that are highly rated in Fiverr and NOT results from beginners.

I just want to mention here that qualified sellers have a lot of orders, so they don't have time to answer the **Buyer Requests** list, which means, most of the sellers that are answering these requests are beginners who don't have orders or they have only few.

✓ **Useful features for buyers:**

➢ Combining Multiples and Gig Extras makes it easy to place large orders (and by the way, this is a new feature published on the Fiverr's blog on November 3, 2013)

➢ Fiverr Goes Mobile – 3M Gigs Now in Your Pocket

- With the brand new iPhone App, you can now buy and work on Fiverr anytime, and anywhere. And for Android users don't worry, Fiverr are working on the Android version.

GIGS SECRETS

Gigs Secrets

✓ **Find the Gigs secrets:**

Actually, many sellers use applications or services that allow them to deliver so fast and without costing them a large investment in time or money. So your job is simply to find these secrets and to use them ☺

➢ **Gig Secret #1: Einstein**

Search results for **'einstein'**

Looking for users containing 'einstein'? Click here ...

Show: Recommended   High Rating   Express Gigs   With Video   New   46 results

I will get Albert Einstein to write on a Chalk Board

I will make Albert Einstein say what ever you want

I will put your message on the blackboard as if it was writen by Eins...

I will place your message written on the board by Einstein

I will make FUNNIEST Einstein video saying your msg in his realistic ...

I will creat an image with your message written on the board by Alber...

I will create a video of Dr Einstein promoting your events or products

I will have your message written on chalkboard by Albert Einstein

I will place your message written on the board by Einstein for $5

- To find the secret behind this Gig I have just copied the Gig's title in Google:

http://www.hetemeel.com/einsteinform.php

FAQ

FAQ

Sellers

✓ **What is the profile image dimensions?**

➢ 250x250 px

✓ **What is the max file size I can send?**

➢ You can deliver up to 150MB in orders (100MB for a single file) and a 30MB limit on message attachments.

✓ **Where to upload bigger files?**

➢ www.dropbox.com

✓ **How I deal with buyers who want to pay me directly?**

➢ You can use this answer *"I prefer to keep it via Fiverr to keep the things organized and secure you and me"*

✓ **Why did I only get paid $4 of a $5 Gig?**

➢ Fiverr must be paid somehow. They receive 20% of every order you make, so $1 per $5

✓ **Why can't I withdraw my money?**

➢ There is a 14 day "clearance" time between when your Gig was marked as "COMPLETED" by the buyer and when you will receive the money in your Fiverr balance; this is to make sure there is satisfaction between the buyer and seller on the order

✓ **How do I add Gig extras?**

➤ Gig extras are available once you reach Level 1. As a no level yet, you are not able to add these extras

✓ **When I update my Gig's title, the URL doesn't change accordingly?**

➤ URL will never change. It stays what you originally named your Gig the first time you created it.

➤ Avoid stating specific quantities in titles ("I will write a **500** word article" etc.) and keep it generic when setting up initially ("I will write an article..."). Once the Gig is active you can then go back to edit the title to be more specific, and the URL now will not change ☺

✓ **Can I change my username OR can I deactivate/close my account?**

➤ You cannot change your username. To deactivate/close your account you have to contact the Customer Support

✓ **My buyer never sent me the order requirements. Can I cancel it?**

➤ When your order is pending requirements for more than 7 days, you'll be able to cancel it by going to the Resolution Center tab at the top of your order page. Fiverrtron will help you from there

✓ **I have an Express Gig, when I request a mutual cancellation will it stop the clock?**

➤ Yes. When you request a mutual cancellation, the clock on your Express Gig will stop. With this, you won't lose your Express status for requesting a mutual cancellation.

✓ **Can I refund an unsatisfied buyer?**

➤ Yes. You can request a mutual cancellation after the order is marked complete and the funds for that order are still in clearing (approx 14 days after the order is marked complete). If your buyer agrees, their feedback will automatically be removed.

✓ **You have a question about anything in Fiverr?**

➤ Contact the Customer Support, they are Fast, Accurate, Reliable

Buyers

✓ **My order is delivered, but it's not what I wanted or I'm not satisfied with the quality of work:**

  ➢ Use the Resolution Center first. In most cases, this issue should be resolved between you and the seller in the order page while allowing Fiverrtron to suggest to reject the delivered work and allow the seller to offer modifications, or even propose a mutual cancellation. If Fiverrtron fails, contact the humans (Customer Support) using the option made available to you in the Resolution Center.

✓ **I don't want to share my delivered work!**

  ➢ That's completely optional. If you want to remove the image or video sent to you by your seller, while rating your experience, simply hover over the thumbnail in the same message box and click on the button in the top right corner of the thumbnail. This allows you to remove the work sample while allowing you to rate your experience with the seller.

✓ **I ordered this Gig by mistake**

  ➢ No worries, the Resolution Center will help you cancel the order. If the seller is waiting for you to reply to their instructions, you can choose the Resolution Center option of "This isn't what I wanted". If the order is already active, ask the seller to use the "I'm having trouble completing this order" to start the cancellation process.

CONCLUSION

Conclusion

✓ I hope you enjoyed **Fiverr V2 Kingdom Formula**.

✓ I will keep updating this e-book according to your suggestions and ideas, so if you have any new creative ideas or suggestions, please feel free to share.

Contact: Support@KingdomFormula.Com

The video course of this e-book

I have made a video course called also "Fiverr V2 Kingdom Formula" based on this CreatSpace's e-book, where I explain in real time how to live in the kingdom of Fiverr.

And as you have already purchased this kindle e-book, you can use the coupon code below to get the video course for only $15, the video course's price without this coupon code is $35:

https://www.udemy.com/fiverr-v2-kingdom-formula/

Coupon code: CreateSpace

www.ingramcontent.com/pod-product-compliance
Lightning Source LLC
Chambersburg PA
CBHW040924180526
45159CB00002BA/602